the Bitter Spirit

The Deadly Effects of Bitterness

PAUL YOUNG

the Bitter Spirit

The Deadly Effects
of Bitterness

PAUL YOUNG

THE BITTER SPIRIT: THE DEADLY EFFECTS OF BITTERNESS
By: Paul Young
Copyright © 2014
GOSPEL FOLIO PRESS
All Rights Reserved

Published by
GOSPEL FOLIO PRESS
304 Killaly St. W.
Port Colborne, ON L3K 6A6
CANADA

ISBN: 9781927521540

Cover design by Danielle Elzinga

All Scripture quotations from the
King James Version unless otherwise noted.

Printed in Canada

Dedicated to my mother,

Norah Alice Young,

who despite the ups and downs of life never
showed a bitter spirit.

A Story...

Louis Zamperini was born in New York in 1917, the son of an Italian immigrant, and grew up in California. As a youngster he got into serious trouble with the police and was rebellious and defiant. However, his attitude changed when he started attending a new school and became a high achiever in athletics.

In 1936 he was part of the American team at the Berlin Olympics and at the age of 19 was the youngest to run in the 5,000 metre race. By finishing the race in eighth position, he became the first American ever to complete the 5,000 metre Olympic race. However, he was not yet in his prime and it was expected that he would hit his peak in time for the 1940 Olympic Games. So he continued running and came very close to breaking the four-minute mile in the late 1930s but then came the Second World War.

He joined the Air Force and was part of a ten-man crew of a Liberator Bomber operating in the Pacific. In 1943 the plane crashed into the sea and forty-seven days later he and another colleague were picked up from a raft that had drifted 2,000 miles into Japanese held waters. In a prisoner-of-war camp he and the others were treated in the most inhumane manner. They had little food and the guards were irrational in their brutality. One guard in particular, known as "The Bird", was dreadfully cruel and meted out awful torture. Louis hated him and hoped one day to kill him. In fact when he returned to the States and married Cynthia he was still haunted with nightmares of "The Bird".

His hope of joining the American team for the 1948 Olympics was dashed when he realized that the clubbing of his legs by "The Bird" had caused him to lose his speed and stamina. At this point he entered a terribly low time, with drinking becoming a problem, arguments with his wife, businesses failing and divorce not far off. However, his wife's demeanour suddenly changed after attending a tent meeting for the preaching of the gospel in downtown Los Angeles. This was a challenge to Louis and he reluctantly went to the tent and heard Billy Graham's message about Jesus. That night he gave his life to the One who loved him and died on a cross for his sins and slept for the first time without the dreadful nightmare of "The Bird".

Later Louis worked as a Youth Director at his church in Hollywood. He also travelled to proclaim the message of the gospel and to give personal testimony to its effectiveness. He was featured on television in 1954 in *This Is Your Life* and his autobiography *Devil at my Heels* came out in 1956. For his eighty-first birthday he ran a kilometre leg with the 1998 Olympic torch at the Winter Olympics at Nagano in Japan. "While he was in Nagano 'The Bird' was tracked down by a reporter. Probably too embarrassed, he refused to see Zamperini. However, the thought of "The Bird" escaping scot-free did not cause Zamperini any bitterness. He forgave because he understood what God's forgiveness had done for him" (*War and Grace*, Don Stephens).

It was not just the length of time that had removed the bitter resentment from his heart but Christ who had cleansed him to the core of his being of all thoughts and feelings of retaliation or revenge. The poison of bitterness had been removed. He had been deeply, miraculously and divinely healed of bitterness. The deadly effects of bitterness had been washed from his mind, heart and soul. For that we should praise God and seek similar cleansing for ourselves.

Another Story...

The date was December 9, 2007 and family life was changed forever for David and Marie Works. They had four delightful daughters: twins Stephanie & Laure, Rachel and Grace. It was Sunday and they were some of the last to leave New Life Church, Colorado Springs, Colorado and had just reached their vehicle. At that moment a young man named Matthew Murray opened fire and killed Stephanie and wounded Rachel and David. Rachel was to die of her wounds soon afterwards in hospital, while David made a long and painful recovery.

Their story is told in *Gone in a Heartbeat* and is deeply moving, especially when they met up with the killer's parents. Matthew Murray had been brought up by gentle, caring, Christian parents, but he struggled with attention-deficit hyperactivity disorder (ADHD). He felt rejected by society and refused to forgive people for slights he felt they had inflicted upon him. His parents realized that "unforgiveness led to his being bitter." Yet they were utterly shocked that his bitterness could take on such savage violence. His shooting rampage might have been even more widespread if an off-duty police officer had not shot him dead.

David and Marie's reaction were as follows: "We would never entirely get over the loss of Stephanie and Rachel. But neither would we give in to despair or bitterness. We would keep moving forward in the present moment and keep looking to find the face of God at every turn." They met Matthew's parents and drew very close to them and when asked, "Why?"

answered, "Well, it's very simple…When you've accepted the Lord as your Saviour, it's one of those requirements. I made a decision 23 years ago, so I didn't have to remake it two months ago—of course I was going to forgive. You have to walk in forgiveness. That's not just a matter of duty; over the years you realize that your only other choice is to be bitter. And I refuse to be bitter."

David Works' words are wise, "Bitterness is what led Matthew Murray over the edge…things festered in his soul. He ultimately chose to settle the score in a frightfully violent way. If I wound up bitter at what he did to our family, wouldn't I be perpetuating another cycle of the same poison? Part of the Christian walk is learning to rise above bitterness."

David and Marie were forced by a terrible crisis to live out what they really believed and truly showed that their faith was genuine. Their lack of bitterness and remarkably forgiving spirit is both a credit to them and to their Saviour whom they love and serve. The Saviour had made them new creations and had given His indwelling Holy Spirit to enable them to react in a worthy way. Bitterness led Matthew Murray to inflict pain, injury, death, destruction and sadness upon people who had done him no harm. True forgiveness led David and Marie to help heal wounds and bring perspective to parents whose son had perpetuated such terrible atrocities. To read the moving account of the two lots of parents meeting is a life-changing experience. Then for the parents of Matthew to meet the lady security officer who had no choice but to gun down their son is a moment of wonder as they unreservedly forgave her and said she did the right thing as so many others might have been killed. Pastor Brady Boyd who witnessed the meetings said, "it is the greatest testimony of forgiveness and redemption that I've ever seen and the highlight of my ministry career."

God grant all of us the same spirit of forgiveness and never let us allow bitterness to spoil our relationships.

Bitterness

Introduction

It is very troubling to witness a bitter person and I have known people in my own family who have become terribly twisted emotionally because they allowed bitterness to flourish within their hearts. My family folklore has described my great grandmother as a deeply bitter woman. For decades she maintained deep resentment towards her daughter, my grandmother. Her unforgiving spirit meant that she was alienated from my grandmother and the reason was simply because she had married an Englishman. Her son-in-law was English and not Welsh! Today this could be considered as racism. The poison of bitterness ran deeply within her, soured her personality, contaminated her life and continually spread its dreadful influence to all with whom she came in contact.

This has given me cause to pause and think about my own reaction and how I deal with the emotional and psychological wounds which have been, or appear to have been, inflicted upon me. As I have reflected on the unfair criticism, unfounded accusations and the imputing of false motives then I have tried to learn to react to these hostile inflictions with tranquility and not with a bitter and resentful spirit. No one could possibly suggest that such a positive reaction to emotional wounds is automatically learnt and it is certainly not easy to overcome negative and bitter feelings. However, we can take heart from those who have left us powerful examples who, with God's help, overcame any tendency towards bitterness. Somehow they conquered the natural tendency to become bitter and were never filled with irritated resentment. Instead they were positive, forgiving and free from the emotional bondage of bitterness.

Fanny J. Crosby

Fanny J. Crosby or Mrs. Van Alstyne (to give her married name) was possibly the most prolific hymn-writer who ever lived. She composed over 8,000 hymns which is a remarkable output of sacred verse by any standard but especially when we remember that she was blind. She was born sighted but at the age of six weeks, due to a doctor's mistake, she became hopelessly blind for the rest of her days.

Her reaction to her blindness was very revealing, she said, "It may have been a blunder on the doctor's part, but it was no mistake of God's. I believe that it was God's intention that I should live in physical darkness so as to be better prepared to sing His praise." Such positive sentiment reveals that she was remarkably free of any bitterness. She had found deep contentment in Jesus Christ and her soul was at peace. She lived to the grand old age of ninety-five and died in 1915.

Her hymns reflect her total trust in the Lord Jesus and her deep desire to praise His name. They include: *All the Way My Saviour Leads Me"*, *"Blessed Assurance, Jesus is Mine"*, *"Praise Him! Praise Him!"*, *"Safe in the Arms of Jesus"* and *"To God be the Glory"*. It seems unlikely that such wonderful expressions of appreciation and worship to God could have been written had bitterness filled her heart. Obviously a number of her hymns have stood the test of time and are still sung in churches to this day. They continue to inspire congregations and enrich true worship to God. We thank God for Fanny Crosby, not just for her inspiring hymns but also for the blessing of her inspiring life.

Gordon Wilson

Gordon Wilson, from Northern Ireland, had the dreadful and deeply traumatic experience of being in Enniskillen on Remembrance Sunday (8th November 1987) when an IRA bomb exploded and rubble buried many people, including him and his 21 year old daughter, Marie. In the terrible darkness and in tremendous pain lying under the debris of destroyed buildings they managed to reach out and hold each other's hands. This is described in moving detail in his book about his daughter which is entitled *Marie*. He recounts how she said, "Daddy, I love you very much." It was the last words she spoke. She died and it broke his heart. However, the book was reviewed by the *Sunday Independent* and the reviewer wrote, "This inspiring man lacks bitterness, praying nightly for those who under cover of darkness planted the bomb."

We could well have understood a measure of bitterness towards those who had caused such havoc and brought so much intense sadness to him and his family. Yet Gordon Wilson found a different response and remained a strong advocate for peace and reconciliation in the troubled province of Northern Ireland and more generally throughout the whole of Ireland. His words in a carefully prepared statement to the IRA were, "…What I meant to do in expressing forgiveness was to set aside personal vengeance and bitterness, which in turn denied the Loyalist paramilitaries any grounds for using bereavement as a pretext for imposing suffering on Nationalists, Catholics, Republicans or IRA members. I wanted no revenge, no bitterness and no grief for other families."

Gordon Wilson became a close friend of Irish President Mary Robinson, took a seat in the Irish Senate (which for a Northerner was very unusual) and worked for peace and reconciliation. He died in 1995.

In both these cases there was a refusal to let bitterness intrude into their hearts. Both the blind hymn writer and the Northern Irish peace activist reached out for God's help to overcome the natural inclination to blame and seek vengeance. They also saw a bigger picture where the name of God could be glorified and the traumatic events they had experienced could make them stronger people to fulfil a higher calling for the collective welfare of other people. We thank God for such people, who show us a better way of dealing with the unfair experiences of life and the terrible, even shocking, things which can intrude into our lives.

Marah

When the nation of Israel journeyed from slavery in Egypt to freedom in the Promised Land, it was an arduous and drawn out pilgrimage. In total it lasted 40 years and this was because the people did not trust the Lord but reacted with dread when they heard of the giants who lived in the land of Canaan. Faith in the Lord could have reduced the journey to a matter of weeks but failure to trust God and instead be dominated by fear caused the journey to be greatly extended.

God prevented them from reaching the Promised Land any earlier to enable the unbelieving generation to die out and a new generation to arise who could enter and conquer the land of promise. Even so God was faithful to His people and fed them with manna (a sort of wafer, known as angels' food) and quail and provided water for them in one of the most inhospitable environments in the world, the Sinai Desert.

We read in Exodus 15, that Israel had travelled for three days and were unable to find any water but eventually they arrived at what became known as Marah. At Marah there was water but it was totally undrinkable because it was bitter. There must have been some terrible impurities in the water that caused the people to spit it out if they even took one mouthful. It was because of its bitter nature that they called the place "Marah" because that name means "bitterness".

However, it wasn't very long before the bitterness was not just in the water but also in the hearts and minds of the people. Their bitterness found expression as they grumbled and complained against Moses, God's chosen leader of Israel. "Where there is resentment and bitterness, there is the poison of destructive criticism." (Stephen Olford). Moses was the focus of the people's destructive criticism but this masked something deeper. Moses was God's chosen leader for the nation and therefore to criticize Moses was, in effect, to criticize and complain against the Lord. Similarly when we are not blessed in the way we think we should be or our prayers are not answered in the manner we expect then we, like Israel, may become bitter, critical and complaining towards the Lord. "It only requires a given set of circumstances, and bitterness—which is really the sin of rebellion and resentment against God—will surface." (Olford)

Moses turned to the Lord in prayer and the Lord revealed the answer to Israel's problems. It was simply that a branch of a nearby tree needed to be thrown into the water. When this was done then the water was transformed from bitterness to sweetness, from something distasteful to something refreshing, from a curse to a blessing. We do not know what kind of tree the branch came from and we have little understanding of how such a miraculous transformation could take place. However, we are convinced that the Lord was the answer to the bitterness in the water and was also the answer to the bitterness in the hearts of the Israelites. It is important to remember that the Lord always has answers to our deepest needs. He has both the power and the love to enable us to conquer the bitterness that can so easily arise in our own hearts.

Israel had experienced physical bitterness, the distasteful sensation of foul, stale, poisonous water. We may have experienced bitter tastes, such as lemon peel, which can be harsh and unpalatable. However physical bitterness is not a particular problem because such foods can easily be avoided. It is the emotion of bitterness which is the much greater problem, the feelings of bitterness which can affect anyone even the most tranquil of persons. Today we may be free of any kind of bitterness (do thank God) but tomorrow we may be engulfed by bitterness because of words spoken to us or about us and of actions done to us, even behind our backs. "The acid test as to whether a person is in true victory is simply this: when the challenge comes, does he turn to the Lord with the faith of contentment, or run from the Lord with the fire of resentment?" (Olford).

CHAPTER ONE

Definition

Essentially bitterness is an attitude of resentment, hostility, irritation and even hatred towards someone or perhaps towards a group of people. The Collins Concise English Dictionary talks of "strong unrelenting hostility or resentment". Hebrews 12:15 speaks of "a root of bitterness" and clearly if that ever develops within the human heart then it will produce the fruit of bitterness. We should "guard against the growth of any 'root of bitterness', an expression which, coming as it does from Deuteronomy 29:18, probably means a person whose heart is turned away from the Lord and who becomes 'a root bearing poisonous and bitter fruit', thereby causing trouble within the Christian community and defiling many besides himself" (*A New Testament Commentary*).

Many years ago I used to teach in a large Comprehensive School in the city of Coventry in England. One member of staff did not get the promotion which he felt he deserved and as he thought about it over the subsequent weeks and months he became deeply resentful. He stopped doing anything which was not contractual, gave up everything that was voluntary and only did what he was obliged to do as a teacher in the school. His whole demeanor became soured and bitter and he constantly talked of how he had been cheated out of what was rightfully his. He had become a bitter person and a root of bitterness was producing its fruit in his life.

Many years later I took the funeral for a man who had lived to the grand old age of 92. Over fifty years earlier he had failed to gain some money from the legacy of a deceased relative. He was denied what he thought was legitimately his. For the next fifty years he talked about that incident with increasing resentment. His family got fed up with his bitterness and wanted him to forget it but he could not forget or let go of his resentment. He would not deal with the root of bitterness in his heart in his earlier life and in the end he could not deal with it. Sadly, he could be described as a bitter and twisted old man. It was a sorrow to see him and listen to the bitter words he spoke and realize that he totally lacked contentment. His life was disturbed in a deep and terrible way, all because of a few hundred pounds. How true it is that *"the love of money is the root of all (kinds of) evil"* (1 Tim. 6:10).

The truth is that a grudge is harder on the one who holds it than on the one against whom it is held. Too often people will not or cannot let go of the pain of the past, and still carry the burdens of things done years ago. It is simply a fact that no matter how long a grudge is nursed, it won't get better. Indeed it can only get worse as it seems to devour a person from the inside. It is often the result of a deep hurt or wound in the spirit through what someone has said or done. There is a feeling of dreadful pain and because thoughts continually focus upon that wound it begins to fester until it becomes infected with the poison of bitterness. This needs to be avoided at all costs because it is so destructive.

Cherie Blair, wife of former British Prime Minister Tony Blair, picks up on this point when she writes about her father in her book, *Speaking for Myself.* Her father had left the family in dire straits when she was very young. She writes, "It was around this time that I renewed contact with my dad, perhaps for the same reasons—the sense that life is too short to hold grudges against the people you love." She seems to have had the good sense not to let bitterness enter her heart over hurts felt deeply from long before. She realized the truth of what someone has written that "to store our memories with a sense of injury is to fill that chest with rusty iron, which God made for refined gold." Thus having bitter resentment in our hearts "is like taking poison and waiting for the other person to die!"

The word "bitterness" and its derivatives "bitter" and "bitterly" occur scores of times in the Bible.

Esau

One such example of a bitter person is Esau. He was denied the hereditary blessing, which he expected to receive as the elder son, from his father Isaac. He lost that blessing because of the treachery of his twin brother Jacob, who deceived their father. When Esau discovered his loss his reaction is vividly described, *"he cried with a great and exceeding bitter cry"* (Gen. 27:34). He was so bitter towards Jacob that he wanted revenge and decided upon murder. We know, as we read the book of Genesis, that Jacob was divinely protected from his brother's bitter anger which, with the passing of years, subsided and eventually the twins were reconciled to each other. Thus time can bring about healing of the soul from the disease of bitterness, if we are willing to let go of the past. Esau became a great and mighty man and was the founding father of the nation of Edom which was strong and powerful, with its people becoming rich and educated. The nation of Edom inhabited the land to the east and south of the Dead Sea.

Naomi

There is a gem of a story in the Old Testament book of Ruth. It commences with tragedy but ends with blessing. Elimelech and his wife Naomi and their two sons Mahlon and Chilion left their ancestral land and home in Bethlehem and moved east to settle, across the River Jordan, in the land of Moab. They moved because there was a famine in their home country. This was hugely ironic as the name "Bethlehem" means "house of bread" and implies fertility of the land and abundance of food. However, the lack of food in the "house of bread" led this family to migrate to Moab and there they settled. The sons married local women named Orpah and Ruth and presumably they looked forward to an enhanced life in their adopted country. Sadly it all went wrong. Firstly, Elimelech died, and was buried in Moab only to be followed to the grave by his two sons who were also buried in their adopted country.

In the grief and tragedy of loss, Naomi decided to return home to Bethlehem. So she crossed back over the Jordan River and arrived in her home town with just one companion, her daughter-in-law: Ruth. The people met her on her return and she insisted that they were no longer to call her "Naomi" but "Mara" which means "bitterness" because she said, *"the Almighty hath dealt very bitterly with me."* She pointed out that she went out full but came back empty. She had left Bethlehem with a husband and sons but had returned with just a daughter-in-law, who was a foreigner from the land of Moab. Her life had become a *"most bitter lamentation"* (Jer. 6:26).

However, Ruth turned out to be an exceptional daughter-in-law. She was hard working, deeply cared for her mother-in-law, showed wonderful integrity, revealed true faith in the Lord and eventually married a wealthy, God-fearing man. Her children became a great delight to Naomi in her old age and her descendants were the most important and influential people in the history of Israel and indeed the world!

One descendant was David, who became the greatest ruler Israel has ever had in the whole of its history even to the modern day. He united the nation, defeated her enemies and extended her borders to the furthest they have ever been. He laid the foundation for a just society and for wealth to be created in the nation. Israel, in David's time, was the most powerful economic, political, military and spiritual force in the Middle East. Even today David is still hailed as the greatest national leader Israel has ever known.

Later, there was an even more famous descendant. He was "great David's greater son". The Lord Jesus Christ was born with the express purpose of dying for our sins on the cross. He died and then rose again and offers salvation, forgiveness and eternal life to all who will trust Him by committing their lives to Him. He is the one who can remove the bitterness of sin from us, if we will only open up our lives to Him and let Him work in us.

Thus Naomi's bitterness was removed and her tears were turned to joy. She found delight through the blessings God bestowed through her daughter-in-law. I think it would be true to say that nobody ever called her "Mara". The bitterness evaporated before the wonderful demonstration of the power and love of God through Ruth who was faithful to both God and Naomi.

Hannah

In the first book of Samuel we read of Hannah who was one of two wives belonging to Elkanah. She was sad and greatly burdened because she had no children, which was compounded by the fact that the other wife, Peninnah, had a number of children. In those days it was a cause of terrible shame and sadness to be barren and childless and Hannah's sorrow was made worse by the cruel remarks that Peninnah made about her. This seems to have been particularly intense on the annual pilgrimages to worship God at the Tabernacle in the city of Shiloh. Eventually, it all got too much for Hannah and she went to the Lord and prayed passionately for a son.

She prayed within her heart and so no words passed her lips. Yet she *"was in bitterness of soul, and prayed unto the Lord, and wept sore"* (1 Sam. 1:10). The best advice for the bitter soul is always to pray to the Lord. For Hannah her prayers were answered in a marvellous and miraculous way and she had a son who became one of the greatest prophets in the history of Israel. His name was Samuel and he led the Israelites in a very turbulent time in their history, heading up the nation spiritually, judicially and politically. He was the last of the judges and first of the prophets. He was one of Israel's most outstanding leaders. Hannah's bitter sorrow was replaced with delightful joy and after Samuel she had other sons and daughters.

Mordecai

Mordecai was the uncle and adoptive father of a Jewish girl named Esther, whose family had been deported to the land of Babylon. In the days of the Persian King Ahasuerus (otherwise known as Xerxes), Esther was chosen to be queen in place of the disgraced and banished Vashti. It was a great privilege for her but her nationality had been kept as a closely guarded secret. Even the King did not know her nationality. An evil man by the name of Haman had gained the king's confidence and in an act of spiteful vindictiveness had persuaded the king to set aside one particular day for the annihilation of the Jewish people throughout the great Persian Empire. This edict was published as a law and fear gripped the Jews. Mordecai went into mourning for his people and *"cried with a loud and a bitter cry"* (Est. 4:1). His bitterness was a reflection of the feelings of the Jews who lived at that time. Many dwelt in the capital city of Shushan and others were scattered throughout the Empire.

Eventually, through the courage and faith of Queen Esther, the tide was turned. The king realized the evil in Haman who was executed, to be replaced by Mordecai as the King's leading adviser. So the people of Israel were miraculously delivered from destruction and the potential persecution was averted by the powerful hand of God. The bitter cry was turned into joyful praise. That transformation is remembered every year by the people of Israel even to this day in the Feast of Purim. This is not a solemn or serious festival but a joyful outpouring of fun and laughter in which all the family take part.

Job

Job was a remarkable man who had a large family, great wealth and high standing in his community. He worshipped God and lived a righteous life. He even offered sacrifices to God on behalf of his children after they had partied, in case they had inadvertently sinned against the Lord. Thus he was a man of very great integrity and deep devotion to God. However, in short order, he lost his children, was stripped of his wealth and lost his credibility in the community. He then lost his health and found himself sitting in ashes scratching his diseased skin with bits of broken pottery. Friends gathered around him but it was simply to criticize him and his motives.

Those friends are known to us as "Job's Comforters". They challenged him to admit to some terrible sin but he refused as he knew the integrity of his own heart. Even his wife was so utterly distraught that she suggested that it would be best for Job to curse God and die. However Job never lost his faith in God and yet his experience was very bitter. He says, *"I will complain in the bitterness of my soul"* (Job 7:11) and again, *"I will speak in the bitterness of my soul"* (Job 10:1). His experience was very bitter and difficult, if not impossible, for him to understand. He did not know that he was a powerful example of faithfulness to unseen angelic beings. In the end, all was restored to him and his bitter experience has proved to be a blessing to all generations who read of it and an especially great encouragement to all those who go through periods of intense suffering and deep trials.

We have seen that many Bible characters experienced the terrible sensation of bitterness. Yet the Scriptures offer solutions and there is no need to remain bitter as ultimately it produces the dark, sinister forces of terrible destruction.

I can think of very little that is worse than a person who is seething with bitterness. There is not much we can do for such a person. They are twisted and churned up inside and constantly their thoughts and conversation turn to and focus upon one event or one person which produced that seed of bitterness. They refused to remove that seed and so it grew to take root in their hearts. The development of root then led to the production of fruit and their thoughts, words and attitude could increasingly be described as bitter. Bitterness summarizes such people. They would not let go before and now it seems that they cannot let go.

The challenge for you and me is to look into our own hearts. There we must remove all seeds: feelings and thoughts of bitterness. We must get rid of them now or perhaps the day will arrive when we will be unable to remove them. Then they will possess us and may ultimately destroy us. Our lives can be deeply and permanently ruined by bitterness.

We need to look at three aspects of bitterness. Firstly we will consider the causes of bitterness, then the consequences of bitterness and finally the cure of bitterness.

CHAPTER TWO

The Causes of Bitterness

Where does bitterness come from? What are its origins? What triggers the bitter reaction, a reaction that can overtake us too easily and dominate us so powerfully? The causes may vary and yet there seem to be some common threads and we will try to uncover some of these as we look at the incident of Simon the Sorcerer, who was an influential and powerful man of Samaria and is mentioned in Acts 8.

In Acts 8:21-23 we read: *"...for thy heart is not right in the sight of God. Repent, therefore, of this thy wickedness, and pray God, if perhaps the thought of thine heart may be forgiven thee. For I perceive that thou art in the gall of bitterness, and in the bond of iniquity."*

These words were spoken by the Apostle Peter to Simon the Sorcerer, who wanted the same power as that exercised by the apostles. Previously, Simon had used magic and demonic power to influence and exercise a certain amount of control over the people of Samaria. Clearly the people were very much afraid of him and were wary of his power. However, following the evangelistic preaching of Philip, the people accepted the message of the Gospel and believed on the Lord Jesus Christ. Thus any demonic hold over them was broken and as a consequence Simon lost his power, status and ability to control people. His authority had been replaced by that of the Lord Jesus. However, he also embraced the message of the Gospel and became a Christian believer, or so it appeared.

Later the apostles Peter and John travelled from Jerusalem to Samaria to undertake an important spiritual task. When they arrived they laid hands upon the new Christian believers who then received the Holy Spirit. Simon, rather foolishly and rashly, offered money to the apostles so that he could also have that same power. He tried to pay for the spiritual ability to call down the Holy Spirit upon anyone on whom he would lay hands. In response, he received a stinging rebuke from the Apostle Peter. The rebuke is so strong that it would appear that Simon's conversion was hardly genuine and he needed to fully repent of his sins. As we review this incident carefully we can uncover some of the underlying causes of the bitterness that filled the heart of Simon.

The Problem of Pride

Clearly, Simon's pride had been dented and his ego had been knocked because he no longer had the same power and influence over the people. No longer was he the important person in the community of Samaria. Christ had superseded him in the eyes of the people. He seems to have reacted with bitter resentment to this loss of status. It was D.L. Moody who wrote, "God sends no one away empty except those who are full of themselves." This seems to have been Simon's experience. Instead of showing a humble spirit, his pride was exposed and he became a bitter person.

Today we may have similar problems caused by pride and egotistical behaviour. We tend to believe that our opinion is very important and therefore we should be highly regarded. This can and does cause problems generally but is particularly destructive in the local church. We must always remember that as Christians, we are subject to a higher authority. All aspects of ministry should be directed by the Lord, through His Holy Spirit and in accordance with His Holy Word.

Thus it is Christ who directs His church and it is He who bestows gifts upon each Christian to enable the fulfilment of His purposes. Some of the gifts bestowed by the Holy Spirit may be more public in their application than others, but they are not necessarily more important. It is too easy to crave the prominence which others may have and feel under-valued that they speak to large congregations and we do not. However each one is answerable to the Lord for the conducting of their life and ministry and for the utilization of their gift. We must always learn contentment in the work of God and be secure in the knowledge of the gifts He has given to us and exercise them for His glory.

We know that the North American evangelist, Charles Finney, had a great ministry of reaching people with the Gospel. Huge numbers attended his meetings and crusades and multitudes accepted the Lord as Saviour. It was a powerful ministry which he exercised and one that was wonderfully anointed by the Lord. However, there was one man, Father Nash, who rarely attended any of Finney's missions but who constantly prayed for the evangelist and his Gospel work. That man sometimes spent whole days in intercession for Charles Finney's preaching. It was constantly upon his heart to uphold the preaching of the Gospel through Charles Finney. One man had the public acclaim while the other was both unheralded and largely unknown. They had different gifts, callings and ministries. Both were vital for the work of the kingdom of God.

The local leadership in a church carries very great responsibilities for the welfare of the flock of God. If that leadership were ever divided then the result is inevitably the division of the church. No church can flourish when it is divided and so elders need to learn the necessity of giving way to each other, of not standing on ego but allowing themselves to change opinion and develop ideas in directions they had not thought of before. This does not apply to the foundations and core truths of the Christian faith which are unalterable but to initiatives, new forms of outreach, fresh ideas for pastoral work and possible changes to programmes. To adapt and change requires deep humility and an ability to subject the ego to the will of God.

So from the experience of Simon the Sorcerer we learn that we need to be careful of personal pride and ego for this can lead to bitterness.

The Problem of Jealousy

Simon had ambition but it was a selfishly jealous ambition. He wanted power and ministry similar to that being exercised by the apostles. He wanted to do what they were doing. It was the writer of the Proverbs who said, *"Wrath is cruel, and anger is outrageous; but who is able to stand before envy?"* (Prov. 27:4). If someone is envious of you then there is very little that you can do about it!

Jealousy can be seen in two ways. Firstly, there is good jealousy which is a godly jealousy for the integrity of God. This is when our hearts are moved to jealously defend the Lord against the blasphemous idolatry so evidently seen in the day in which we live. It is to feel the pain of hurt on behalf of the Lord as His Name is demeaned and denigrated by all sorts of people, especially many in the entertainment and media industry.

Secondly, there is **bad jealousy** which is a selfish feeling of resentment at some perceived injury or slight inflicted on us personally. It is a covetous desire for a position of influence, for recognition and for appreciation, which we feel is given to others but is denied to us. It is ambition gone selfishly and hopelessly wrong. Frequently, bitterness is associated with jealousy.

The Apostle James wrote these words, *"...ye have bitter envying and strife in your hearts"* (Jas. 3:14). Jealousy and wrong ambition can be harboured in the heart and it can fester until it produces deep bitterness in the soul. Someone has written, "In counselling Christians, we frequently see bitterness associated with jealousy. The examples include successful attorneys who envy the ability of their colleagues, Bible College and seminary students consumed with jealousy toward fellow students...pastors or missionaries envious of others who have seen outward evidences of success" (*How to Beat Burnout*).

So from the experience of Simon the Sorcerer we understand that we need to be careful of jealousy and selfish ambition because these can lead to bitterness, which will bring the condemnation of the Lord.

Outside the Will of God

We can almost hear the thundering words of the Apostle Peter to Simon the Sorcerer, *"Thy heart is not right in the sight of God"* (Acts 8:21). Simon's heart, consumed as it was with pride, jealousy, selfishness and false ambition, clearly revealed that he was not right with God. He was not pursuing the will of God in his life. There was falseness about the man, a hypocrisy, which still pursued worldly aims at the expense of his relationship with God.

If ever we entertain any bitter feelings and attitudes then we must be under no illusion, we are outside the will of God. We are being disobedient to our God and will be so out of touch with the Lord that we will not enjoy His presence or His blessing. The Spirit of God will be grieved and we will be unable to serve the Lord effectively. We will be robbed of the joy of the Lord and our love will quickly turn to hatred. We will lose the desire to pray and find no delight in reading the Word of God. The bitter heart is a heart that ruins the Christian. If Simon had failed to repent of his bitterness then he would have been unable to serve the Lord or to enjoy any sort of fellowship or have any real relationship with the Saviour.

So from the experience of Simon the Sorcerer we learn that bitterness indicates that we are outside the will of God.

The Result of Wickedness

Peter describes Simon's request as *"thy wickedness"* (Acts 8:22). The bitter heart is a wicked heart. Bitter feelings are sinful feelings. The bitter attitude is an evil attitude. It can easily lead to bondage and enslavement. Indeed, Peter goes on to say, *"I perceive that thou art in the gall of bitterness"* (Acts 8:23). Simon had not actually found freedom and victory over sin through faith in Christ. His profession of faith seems to have been a pseudo-trust and he was still very much in bondage to sin. The bitterness he exhibited indicated very clearly that he was still in his sinful condition before God and therefore needed to repent and truly trust Christ as Saviour for the forgiveness of sin.

The causes of bitterness may vary but bitterness is an evil and a sin against God. We need to search our heart continually to isolate and remove all bitterness from our spirit, because it is a most destructive influence upon the life of any individual, especially those who are Christians.

CHAPTER THREE

The Consequences of Bitterness

Bitterness is not just one isolated thought or one stray feeling of resentment which we may experience when we are hurt or wounded in our spirit by words or actions. Bitterness is something which is compounded and it does not stay as just a feeling or as a single thought. The seed of resentment may be small but if it is not rooted out then it grows and eventually our actions, words, behaviour and way of life will be dominated and motivated by bitter feelings and thoughts.

There may be one particular person and whenever we see that person or are in that person's company bitterness fills our heart. We may find it difficult to speak to that person and we try to avoid him or her at all times. We make every attempt to isolate or insulate our lives from that individual. We want to alienate such a person or persons, maybe we are even rude to them and want to leave them out in the cold as far as our social circle is concerned. We don't care about them, we gossip 'about them, take every opportunity to criticize and disparage them. We constantly recall all that is bad about them, all the hurt (real or imagined) which they have heaped upon us in the past. The effects are devastating.

The first effect is upon us. We become cold in heart towards God, have difficulty praying and serving the Lord and end up as weak, worldly and failed Christians. So the effect of bitterness has a deep impact upon our own lives and that impact is always negative. William Shakespeare wrote, "Heat not a furnace for your foe so hot that it do singe yourself." Also Dale Carnegie said, "Wouldn't our enemies rub their hands with glee if they knew that our hate for them was exhausting us, making us tired and nervous, ruining our looks, giving us heart trouble and probably shortening our lives?" We are, therefore, well warned that bitterness in our heart will badly affect and even destroy us in some way or other.

The second effect is upon the person to whom we feel bitterness. Such a person can lose esteem in the eyes of others because of our words and thus his or her integrity is weakened. He cannot truly realize his potential for God because of what we might have said about him. Also it may be that the effect of our bitterness can cause physical ailments for other people.

My sister died at the relatively young age of forty-nine. I well remember that a close family member became deeply bitter towards her and this came as a 'bolt out of the blue' when he said he wanted nothing more to do with her and wanted no more contact with her. She was deeply shocked, dreadfully hurt and never recovered emotionally. In a matter of months she was diagnosed with cancer and died seven weeks later. The effect of those bitter words may have had nothing to do with the cancer but they certainly weakened and demoralized my sister to the extent that she was less able to deal positively with her illness.

It is true that "invisible emotional tension in the mind can produce striking visible changes in the body, changes that can become serious and fatal." (*None of These Diseases,* S.I. McMillen). We, therefore, need to take great care before we utter words which can wound and hurt other people. We certainly do not want to be the cause of illness or even death in others. May God in His mercy preserve and protect us from such destructive bitterness.

The third effect is upon the church. Bitterness can divide a church. This is made clear by the apostle James who mentions the word "strife". Christian unity is fragile and my bitter feelings can weaken, undermine or even destroy it. Certainly my bitter attitude and words can utterly ruin unity and when unity is destroyed in the local church then the potential for blessing is diminished or even gone altogether. The ability to worship God is undermined by division and so division needs to be avoided at all costs. Thus we need to crush anything that could be negative and that includes bitterness.

The early Christian work in Serampore, India, where William Carey with his colleagues Marshman and Ward achieved so much in the early nineteenth century, was marred to some extent in their last years by division caused by some new recruits. John Appleby writes, "Dr. Johns became very bitter, feeling that Serampore should have fought more vigorously for his retention in Bengal...his bitterness was to be a cancer that infected future recruits to the work... and knowledge of this made Carey quite ill" (*I Can Plod*). The bitterness which was allowed to fester in the heart of Dr. Johns adversely affected the work of the Gospel in India and had a negative effect upon the health of longstanding missionaries. It is so right to describe such bitterness as a cancer because if not crushed then it grows as a dreadful malignancy upon the soul and creates havoc with Christian friendship and unity.

Fourthly if we give way to bitterness then it can lead to further sins. It can become the first step in serious backsliding and its effect upon others can be extensive. If a Christian gives in to bitterness and leaves the church then other believers can become deeply discouraged. Also, such actions can cause non-believers to have a disincentive to take any interest in the glorious Gospel of Jesus Christ. Bitterness spoils our integrity as individuals and it spreads like some dreadful disease in a body or some awful weed in a garden, and so can cause "*many (to) be defiled*" (Heb. 12:15).

When this happens the consequences can be dire. A church where I have preached many times found itself with a person who was filled with bitterness towards one of the elders. No one was really sure what was the cause of the bitterness but its effects were blatantly obvious to all. On the days when there was a communion service the elders would dispense the bread and wine to the congregation. If that particular elder was offering the sacraments to the bitter person she steadfastly refused to take it. She would take it if offered by another elder but not that particular one. Attempts were made to bring about reconciliation but it was all hopeless. The bitterness intensified and eventually she left the church. Today that church is closed and the building has been purchased by a property developer. Nothing we do or say is ever in isolation. It always has its consequences and so bitterness needs to be crushed as soon as possible.

CHAPTER FOUR

The Cure for Bitterness

Sometimes people approach me and say, "It's alright for you living the Christian life because you are a full-time preacher!" They must think that I have some charmed spirituality which lifts me above the everyday struggles which lesser mortals have! However, the truth is that if anyone has problems in this area of bitterness then I certainly do. Like everyone else I have experienced the wounds and hurts inflicted by others. Like others, too, I have tried to cover up and pretend that all was well. I also have put up a positive front and gone through the motions that everything was alright when deep down I knew that all was not right.

There have been times when I have felt bitterness towards a fellow-Christian, usually over something they said to me or about me. To pretend is not an answer and I am well aware that a bitter spirit can destroy my ministry for God. Thankfully God has given me a wonderful wife who on more than one occasion has pulled me out of the morass of bitterness into which I was sinking. She has enabled me to see the bigger picture, to gain a better perspective and to overcome the bitter trend within me. I thank God for my wife and the positive input she has upon my ministry.

How Do We Conquer Bitterness?

The process is not easy and there are no simplistic answers and no straightforward formula to follow. It is enormously hard work and requires continual diligence to escape the fatal clutches of a bitter spirit. The following are some suggestions, which if followed, should help us to conquer the problem of bitterness.

Clear Sightedness

We should view the other person, the one to whom we are bitter, as someone who is deeply loved by God. Here is someone whom God loves so much that He sent His Son to die for that person. If God loves that person unreservedly then so must I. That love cannot simply be worked up as a human sentiment but is a deep work of the Holy Spirit in our lives which produces the fruit of love. So this love must flow into and through our hearts from a divine source, namely from God Himself. As we yield our lives ever more fully to Christ, then His Spirit can fill us and produce the fruit of love in our hearts, even towards people we may find to be very difficult.

Repentance

The Apostle Peter instructed Simon the Sorcerer to *"repent therefore of this thy wickedness"* (Acts 8:22). Simon needed to exercise a change of heart and outlook. He required a fundamental change in his life and behaviour. If we are ever to conquer bitterness then there must be a deep desire in our hearts to leave it, as Ephesians 4:31, NIV indicates when it says, *"get rid of all bitterness"*. This is repentance. It is letting go, renouncing, getting rid of, wanting to be relieved of and driving away all feelings of bitterness. It is the desire to be like the Saviour in our attitude, feelings and motivation.

Prayer

Again we read the instruction of Peter to Simon the Sorcerer, *"pray God, if perhaps the thought of thine heart may be forgiven."* So coupled with repentance was the need to pray out the bitterness in his heart. For us it means staying on our knees in genuine prayerfulness until we have allowed God to deal with the bitterness within us. It is to pray until we have left the bitterness at the feet of Jesus, until we have the knowledge of God's great forgiveness and cleansing.

Here we see the difference between "saying prayers" and "truly praying". The difference is between the formality of saying prayers and the reality of true intercession with God. True prayer is more than just words—it is from the heart and is a clear connection with the living God. We must be careful never to allow our prayers to become simply ritualistic and therefore meaningless. Thus in terms of getting rid of something like bitterness there is need to be real with God and to remain on our knees in prayer until we have encountered God and experienced His deliverance and blessing. Ultimately true prayerfulness is the answer to overcoming a bitter and resentful spirit.

Read the Bible

The daily and systematic reading of the Word of God is vital in the washing away of such things as bitterness. The simple activity of focusing upon God's message is in itself a cleansing process. It is described as the washing of water by the Word. Also as we read the Word of God we come across inspiring examples of people who did not allow themselves to become victims of bitterness and who ultimately achieved outstanding things for God. Also we read of those who failed to gain victory over bitterness and thus became examples of what not to be.

Joseph

We have a wonderfully positive example in the Old Testament book of Genesis. Joseph was his father Jacob's favourite son. He was given a coat of many colours to indicate his favoured position. This caused his brothers to be jealous of him. Also he was given prophetic dreams from God about his future status which would make him ruler over his people. This made his brothers angry. Joseph was ripped from his father's household by those jealously angry brothers, who wanted to kill him but instead sold him to slave traders.

The slave traders in turn sold him to Potiphar, a leading soldier in Egypt and Joseph, through conscientious hard work and personal integrity, became the chief man in Potiphar's household. Then Joseph was falsely accused and found himself chained and in prison and it had all started with jealous brothers. We could well understand any bitter thoughts and feelings he might have harboured, even a desire for revenge if ever he met up with them. However, there is absolutely no evidence that he had such thoughts, even for a moment.

His trust in God was both total and remarkable and when the day came that he could have exacted revenge, as Prime Minister of Egypt, he did not. The brothers thought he would punish them for the dreadful way they had treated him but in an act of godly graciousness he forgave them and pointed out that though their actions were meant for evil, God had been there all the time and had arranged it all for good. They had tried to destroy his life but God had used that life to bless and save many people, including his own family, from death by starvation. Throughout his trials, disappointments, unfair treatment and false accusations there seems to have never been a moment's bitterness in Joseph; just a simple and straightforward trust in God which made him assume that all would work out right in the end. Such a story inspires us to allow God to deal with our bitter and twisted hearts.

The Older Brother

In contrast with Joseph we have the negative example of the older brother in the parable that Jesus told in Luke 15. The parable is traditionally known as the "Prodigal Son" or the "Lost Son". There was a man who had two sons and the younger decided that he wanted to leave home and the hard work of the farm and enjoy the bright lights of a distant land. His father gave him the portion of inheritance which would have been his due and the son left. In course of time, after a riotous lifestyle, the son was penniless and friendless. His only recourse was to find work and the only work was caring for pigs (which was abhorrent to Jewish sensibilities), his only wage was to eat the same pods that the pigs were given. Eventually he came to himself and journeyed home to his father. He wanted to say 'Sorry' and asked for no special favours but would have been glad to be employed as a slave in his father's house.

The father looked out, saw his son coming home and shedding all dignity ran to his son, embraced him and welcomed him home with a kiss, a new coat, sandals for his feet (as only slaves went barefoot) and a tremendous party with good food and music. However, when the older son came home from working in the fields and was told that the younger brother was in the house and a welcome home party was in full swing he refused to join in the merriment. He revealed a bitter heart which produced vindictive accusations both against his brother and against his father who had welcomed the Prodigal. He complained that he had worked hard, obeyed all instructions and had never wasted a penny yet he had been given no party, however, his brother, who wasted everything he ever had, was being given a great feast of joy. To him it seemed so unfair and undeserving. Bitterness spoiled the party and hurt his father. It caused him to sulk and be a selfish killjoy. Yet the truth was that the entirety of his father's wealth belonged to him and still he could not spare some kindness for his returning, repentant brother. He simply demonstrated bitter resentment towards him.

If Joseph is an example of someone in Scripture to be imitated then the older brother's reaction is an example which must not be replicated.

Have a Purpose in Life

It is both instructive and sad to read the autobiography of Benazir Bhutto. She was born in Pakistan and was part of a privileged and wealthy family. She was the oldest child of Ali Bhutto who was Prime Minister of the country. She was an intelligent person who was educated at Harvard and Oxford Universities and also found herself at her father's side at a number of important political events. Sadly her father was overthrown in a political coup, was falsely accused and wrongly imprisoned. He had introduced a new constitution to the country that was democratic with safeguards for the poor, for women and for minority groups. He was executed on the orders of General Zia.

Benazir found herself victimized by the regime. She endured long periods of house arrest and then imprisonment in filthy conditions and often in isolation. She was exiled for a number of years and had to cope with the death of her brother who was also, in all likelihood, murdered on the orders of Zia. Eventually she overcame illness, exile and threats to return in triumph to Pakistan and be overwhelmingly elected as Prime Minister in 1988. She was just thirty-five years of age and the first woman leader of a Muslim nation. She in turn was overthrown, only to be elected a second time and again overthrown by a military coup.

Tragically she was assassinated in 2007 while campaigning for re-election. She was a brave and determined woman who wanted to help the poor and keep extremism at bay.

Many thought she only campaigned to avenge her father's death but she wrote, "You can't be fuelled by bitterness. It can eat you up, but it cannot drive you. The task—my motivation—remained the same: to return Pakistan to a democracy through fair and impartial elections." Her potential for bitterness was overcome by an overriding purpose in life. She saw her life's work not as a personal vendetta but as service to her people and especially the needy. She constantly worked for the goal of raising the literacy levels of her people and her government built schools, gave human rights to women, to minority religious groups and generally empowered the poor against exploitation. She also kept the country free from the fanatical extremism that now affects so much of Pakistan and indeed the world.

Christians must always have a vision of the world which incorporates its need of the Gospel of God's saving grace. Thus the purpose for God's people is the work of evangelism in which we share the glorious message of Christ. This is a work of care and love to a hurting world and it should motivate us and lift us above our petty jealousies, pride and bitterness. When we see and understand what God's will is for our lives, then anything that distracts or diverts us from that aim must be jettisoned. If we are aimless we can become bitter but when we know our purpose in life then we have no time for bitterness as we pursue that purpose with every fibre of our being.

This may not be straightforward as we can so easily be infected with the poison of bitterness as difficulties and trials arise in our lives. Someone has written, "As difficulties come, let us make sure that we become better and not bitter Christians." We should see our lives as being purified by trials so that we can better serve the Lord and fulfil His purpose for our lives.

Look at Christ on the Cross

As the nails were driven into the hands and feet of the Lord Jesus by rough, uncaring Roman soldiers, Jesus reacted in a different way from most people when they were being crucified. Usually the reaction would be to curse and shout abuse at the executioners or at least to look at them with hate-filled eyes but no such bitter reaction came from the Saviour. His words reveal no sense of bitterness, resentment or hatred. He says, *"Father, forgive them; for they know not what they do"* (Luke 23:34).

If anyone had cause to be bitter, then He had. If anyone had a genuine reason to express bitter anger, then He did. He had been unfairly accused. The charges were not genuine but trumped up. The court had not upheld the normal rules of

Roman justice and legal integrity but the magistrate Pontius Pilate had given way to mob rule and made a political decision. He felt that to crucify Jesus would quieten the crowds and bring an end to any disturbance in the city of Jerusalem. How wrong he was! Jesus had cause to feel bitter but exhibited no bitterness at all. It is a powerful example to us because we have never suffered the unfairness He experienced and yet too easily we can become very bitter and resentful.

Forgiveness is a decision we make and though we can't forget the hurts inflicted upon us we can say, "I forgive". This needs to be repeated every day and at the same time we need to ask the Lord for help to make the words meaningful and effective in our lives. With His grace and help we can truly be forgiving people who do not let bitterness ruin both our relationships with other people and also our relationship with the Lord.

Forgiveness is the antidote for bitterness. In May 2008 Rosimeiri Boxall, at the age of nineteen, committed suicide by jumping from a window. She was driven to this desperate act by the bullying of two acquaintances who had made her life a misery by slapping and punching her and spraying deodorant into her face. In court they were convicted and found guilty of causing her death by manslaughter. Rosi was the adopted daughter of Rev. Simon Boxall and his wife Rachel. They deeply loved Rosi and their loss was enormous but they could say: "We are sure that she is now safe in God the Father's arms."

Her parents were also quoted as saying: "We continue to pray for those who are responsible for Rosi's death. We want them to know that we forgive them. That does not mean that what they did doesn't matter, of course it does." They added, "Forgiveness means that we refuse to be shackled by bitterness and our prayer is that forgiveness will allow the girls to be released from the burden of what they've done so that they can even now grow into the sort of people that God intended them to be" (*Evangelicals Now*). It is hard to imagine such a response but with Christ's help it can be achieved. So "forgiveness is loving those who hurt us or can only give us a little love in return… it allows us to come together in non-manipulative and non-demanding ways" (*Encountering Missionary Life and Work*). This is so important if we are to overcome the poison of bitterness.

We must never let bitterness weaken the quality of our personal Christian lives. We must not let bitterness ruin the work of our church life. We need the fullness of the Holy Spirit in our lives through a close fellowship with the Saviour so that we can experience the holy contentment which is found in doing the will of God. Corrie ten Boom, who had survived the horrors of a Nazi concentration camp in which her sister, Betsy, died, wrote these words: "It was 1947…I had come from Holland to defeated Germany with the message that God forgives. It was a truth they needed most to hear in that bitter, bombed out land" (*Tramp for the Lord*). She overcame all feelings of bitterness which could have haunted her life because of the cruel actions of concentration camp guards and German military personnel. She reflected in a wonderful way the forgiving attitude of her Lord and Saviour, Jesus Christ.

Bitterness will always destroy and so we must wage war upon it and never let it defeat us. The battle at times is hard but with the Lord's help we can know victory and follow the Lord's instruction through the words of the Apostle Paul, *"And be ye kind one to another, tenderhearted, forgiving one another, even as God for Christ's sake hath forgiven you"* (Eph. 4:32).

Susanne Geske

Susanne came from Germany the daughter of parents who divorced when she was five years old. At the age of twenty she left home and in a remarkable way came to faith in Christ. She went on to Bible College and did some months of training on a mission trip to Africa in the country of Zaire (now known as Congo). She eventually married a very shy and unassuming man named Tilmann Geske. Their family was completed with three children, two daughters and a son. Eventually they went to serve the Lord in Malatya in Eastern Turkey. Tilmann set up a business, with an office in the town, and they tried to communicate the love of Christ with local Turkish people on a personal basis. Then in April 2007 Tilmann and two colleagues were tortured and killed in their office. The terrible crime still echoes in Turkey to this day as the legal process drags on.

The shock for Susanne was overwhelming but she maintained a steady poise and quiet determination in the face of this dreadful event. She was able to say, "I believe that Jesus went to the cross to forgive all our sins and on the cross He forgave those who were taking His life, saying: 'Father forgive them, for they do not know what they are doing.' So I am going to forgive the people who took the life of my husband because truly they did not know what they were doing. I am going to stay here to show them that I forgive them." Her love for Christ, her love for people and her love for the Gospel have driven out any bitterness that might have taken root. Her loss is incalculable but her love is a true and wonderful reflection of the love of Jesus Christ, her Lord and Saviour.

Just As I Am

She was an embittered woman, Charlotte Elliott of Brighton, England. Her health was broken, and her disability had hardened her. "If God loved me," she muttered, "he would not have treated me this way."

Hoping to help her, a Swiss minister named Dr. Cesar Malan visited the Elliotts' on May 9, 1822. Over dinner, Charlotte lost her temper and railed against God and her family in a violent outburst. Her embarrassed family left the room and Dr. Malan, left alone with her, stared at her across the table.

"You are tired of yourself, aren't you?" he said at length. "You are holding to your hate and anger because you have nothing else in the world to cling to. Consequently, you have become sour, bitter and resentful."

"What is your cure?" asked Charlotte.

"The faith you are trying to despise."

As they talked, Charlotte softened. "If I wanted to become a Christian and to share the peace and joy you possess," she finally asked, "what would I do?"

"You would give yourself to God just as you are now, with your fightings and fears, hates and loves, pride and shame."

"I would come to God just as I am? Is that right?"

Charlotte did come just as she was. Her heart was changed that day. As time passed she found and claimed John 6:37 as a special verse for her, "*...and him that cometh to Me I will in no wise cast out.*"

Several years later, her brother, Rev. Henry Elliott, was raising funds for a school for children of poor clergymen. Charlotte wrote a poem, and it was printed and sold across England. The leaflet said: *Sold For the Benefit of St. Margaret's Hall, Brighton: Him That Cometh To Me I Will In No Wise Cast Out.* Underneath was Charlotte's poem – which has since become the most famous invitational hymn in history.

Just as I am, without one plea,
But that Thy blood was shed for me,
And that Thou bidd'st me come to Thee,
O Lamb of God, I come! I come!

Just as I am, though tossed about
With many a conflict, many a doubt,
Fightings and fears within, without,
O Lamb of God, I come! I come!

(The above was taken from *Preacher's Sourcebook of Creative Sermon Illustrations* by Robert J. Morgan)

"Charlie, it's Gone!"

One night in China, Southern Baptist missionary C.L. Culpepper stayed up late for devotions, but as he tried to pray he felt like stone. Finally he asked, "Lord, what is the matter?"

I had opened my Bible to Romans 2:17-21a. It seemed the Apostle Paul was speaking directly to me when he said, *"Now you, if you call yourself a Jew* (Christian); *if you rely on the law and boast in God; if you know his will and approve of what is superior because you are instructed by the law; if you are convinced that you are a guide for the blind, a light for those who are in the dark, an instructor of the foolish, a teacher of little children, because you have in the law the embodiment of knowledge and truth – you, then, who teach others, do you not teach yourself?"*

The Holy Spirit used this verse like a sword to cut deeply into Culpepper's heart. He said, "You are a hypocrite! You claim to be a Christian! What have you really done for Christ? The Lord said those who believed on Him would have rivers of living waters flowing from their inmost being! Do you have that kind of power?"

Culpepper awakened his wife, and they prayed into the night. The next morning at a prayer meeting with fellow workers, he confessed to pride and spiritual impotence, saying his heart was broken. The Holy Spirit began to so convict the others of sin that they could hardly bear it. Their faces grew pale, then they began to cry and drop on their knees or fall prostrate on the floor. Missionaries went to missionaries confessing wrong feelings toward one another. Preachers, guilty of envy, jealousy and hatred, confessed their sins to one another.

The revival spread through the seminary, the schools, the hospital, and the area churches. Perhaps the deepest impact was made on Culpepper's friend Wiley B. Glass, a much respected missionary. As Glass sat in the meetings, a man's face came before him and God seemed to be asking him about his attitude toward that man. Glass had hated the man for many years, and suddenly the Holy Spirit brought him under deep conviction.

In great anguish, Glass went to Culpepper, fell on his shoulder, and said, "Charlie, pray for me!" Both men went to their knees, but Glass was so distressed he couldn't express his problem. He was pale as death and kept groaning in his anxiety. He was joined in prayer then and prayer was made for him several times during that day and the next. In the evening of the second day he came running and threw his arms around his colleague. "Charlie, it's gone!" he exclaimed. Charlie said, "What's gone?" He replied, "That old root of bitterness." He then spoke of an event thirty years earlier, before he came to China, when a man had insulted his wife. The insult had made him so angry he felt that he could kill the man if ever he saw him again. He realized a called servant of God should not feel this way, and it had bothered him for years. Finally he just turned the man over to God. When the Holy Spirit began working in his heart during that week, the question came," Are you willing for that man to be saved?" He answered, "Lord, I'm willing for You to save him...just keep him on the other side of heaven!" Finally, he came to the place where he said, "Lord, if that man is alive, and if I can find him when I go on furlough, I will confess my hatred of him and do my best to win him for You."

When he reached that decision, the Lord released the joys of heaven to his soul, and he was filled with love and peace. He became a more effective preacher for the Lord, and during the next few years he led hundreds to Christ (*Preacher's Sourcebook*).

Bishop Festo Kivengere

Bishop Kivengere lived in Uganda during the turbulent years of the brutal regime of Idi Amin. Amin was one of the most ruthless dictators ever to hold high office in Africa. He killed many, many people and particularly persecuted the Christian Church as he espoused Islam in an attempt to gain financial support from oil-rich Arab countries. Archbishop Luwum was killed possibly by Amin himself but certainly on his orders. Luwum was Kivengere's friend and colleague in Christian ministry in Uganda. Kivengere had to flee across the border for his life and only just managed to escape Amin's henchmen. He eventually arrived in Britain and found exile in London.

He was comparatively safe while his fellow countrymen were hounded and destroyed by Amin's troops. He had to face his own attitude to Amin and find out what God required of him in response. He wrote: "Peace is not automatic...It always comes when hearts are exposed to the love of Christ. But this always costs something. For the love of Christ was demonstrated through suffering, and those who experience that love can never put it into practice without some cost. I had to face my own attitude towards President Amin and his agents. The Holy Spirit showed me that I was getting hard in my spirit, and that my hardness and bitterness toward those who were persecuting us could only bring spiritual loss. This would take away my ability to communicate the love of God, which is the essence of my ministry and testimony. So I had to ask for forgiveness from the Lord, and for grace to love President Amin more...This was fresh air for my tired soul. I knew I had seen the Lord and been released: love filled my heart."

Conclusion

The Second Century Roman Emperor Marcus Aurelius has been described as "the philosopher-king of the Roman Empire". He wrote a book entitled, *Meditations*. "The general sentiment of the *Meditations* is that overreaction and lingering bitterness are the most damaging responses to life's iniquities. 'If you are pained by any external thing, it is not this that disturbs you, but your own judgment of it,' he writes. 'And it is in your own power to wipe out this judgment now'" (Simon Seberg Montefiore, *101 World Heroes*).

George MacDonald, whose genre of writing was the fountainhead for such literary luminaries as C.S. Lewis and J.R.R. Tolkien, had many problems in his life. "With eleven children, MacDonald didn't always find it easy to put bread on the table but, in spite of problems with finance and his health, there was no bitterness. He rejoiced in the goodness of God" (*3000 Quotations from the writings of George MacDonald* by Harry Verploegh). Somehow he was able to deal with bitterness and, in the words quoted above of Marcus Aurelius, found the "power to wipe out" the inner judgments that produce the corrosive effects of bitterness.

Bitterness is a deeply destructive emotion. It can develop in our spirits like infection in a physical wound. It has the potential to immobilize us in our work, destabilize us in our thinking and destroy our relationships with other people. It can make us ineffective and useless for God's service and could undermine the work of our church and its standing in our community. A bitter reaction will always undermine the integrity of the Gospel because the Gospel is a message that conquers bitterness. The Lord Jesus took all our bitterness on the cross where the ultimate price for sin was paid by Him. So in Christ we can find release from the oppressive bondage that bitterness produces. May God grant us the grace to always leave bitterness at the feet of the Saviour so that we can live life unburdened by the weight of a bitter spirit which ultimately will cause the most damage to ourselves.

I hope you understand that this short book was written out of a burdened heart which wants to bring relief to all who suffer from bitterness whether they are those who wound or the afflicted. Bitterness is a poison that saps the soul of contentment and joy, which ruins and destroys fellowship, friendships and relationships, and obscures the love and grace of God. May it have no place in our experience. We must work hard to make sure it is removed far from us.

Other Books by Paul Young

*The End of a Nation: Studies of Obadiah**

*The Friend Abraham and the Promise of God Isaac**

*Understanding the Bible**
Inspiration, Inerrancy & Interpretation

Outreach Through the Local Church
Problems and needs

*The New Age Movement: A Cunningly Devised Fable**
A detailed look at this movement

Raging Waves: Studies in the Epistle of Jude

*Cunningly Devised Fables**
A look at 13 cults and religions and an overview of their characteristics

The Challenge of Revival
A look back at the 1904 Welsh Revival and a challenge for us in the present

The Diary of a Prophet
Studies in the book of Haggai

A Glimmer of Light
Studies in the book of Lamentations

All books available from:
31, Fairmeadows, Maesteg, South Wales, CF34 9JL

*Books available from **GOSPEL FOLIO PRESS**
www.gospelfolio.com • (905)-835-9166

www.ingramcontent.com/pod-product-compliance
Lightning Source LLC
Chambersburg PA
CBHW060541030426
42337CB00021B/4384